Messages for the Soul

By Tanaaz Chubb

www.foreverconscious.com

How to Use this Book:

This book is designed to offer you drops of wisdom, affirmations and mantras for a little daily pick me up.

Flip to a random page in the book or read it in order, whatever you choose know that each message is being delivered to your soul as an opportunity to awaken your consciousness.

You can use the mantras throughout the day as a way to remind and recharge your soul.

In times of need you can also ask a question and then open a page in the book to see what answer your soul has for you.

The winds have spoken, you must not rest here. Change is inevitable. Change is growth. Embrace this cycle and know that you can choose to steer it in the direction of your choice.

"I welcome in change and know that it is necessary for my growth. I know that I have the power to navigate through these changes so they may influence my life in a positive way."

Sometimes the smallest acts of kindness can have the biggest effects. Today, practice kindness with all that you meet, be compassionate towards life and watch how life responds in kind.

"Today I will open my heart to accepting and appreciating everyone and everything. I will walk through the world with kindness and compassion knowing that the world needs more of it."

Your heart is trying to speak, are you listening? Your heart holds its own type of wisdom that is different to the wisdom of the mind and the body. Tune into the smooth hum of your heart and see what it is asking from you today.

"I am open to the Divine messages of my heart and I am ready to hear its message. I trust my intuition and know that my heart will guide me."

How far can you run before you start to feel lost? Running away from your problems and your pain is no longer serving you. Today, you must embrace all that you feel and accept its presence in your life. It is only through accepting that you can truly start the path of healing.

"Today, I accept where I am and how I am feeling. I accept all that has happened in my life and I accept that this is where I am meant to be right now."

Your angels and spirit guides are working with you today in order to help you achieve your goals. Reach out to your guardian angels and know that you will be guided towards your highest path.

"My angels and spirit guides are with me today for my highest good and I am open to hearing their Divine messages as I walk my highest path."

Do you feel the love that you have for yourself radiating through your being? Can you look in the mirror, deep into your eyes and say to yourself- *"I Love You"*? Today is the perfect day to practice this.

"I honor my body, mind and soul and treat it with love and respect. Everyday I am finding new ways to Love myself more. I love you."

Happiness must be created, it is not something to be found. Today, aim to create happiness and joy in all that you do no matter how big or how small. Allow yourself the opportunity to create as many moments of happiness as you can.

"I am creating more happiness and joy in my life by opening my heart and mind to all the amazing and limitless possibilities that life has in store for me."

Life is sometimes turned upside down and inside out in order to change your perspective and give you a different way of looking at things. Sometimes when you change the way you look at things, the things themselves change.

"Today I open my eyes to seeing things differently. I welcome in new perspectives and ideas and know that every day holds an opportunity to learn something new."

Peace must be found inside your soul in order to proceed further. Still your heart, body and mind and allow calmness and relaxation to flow into your life. If things are bothering you, shelve them for now and focus instead on relaxing.

"Today I allow myself to be just as I am. I allow myself to feel relaxed and at peace with my situation and I know that clarity will come when I allow stillness to wash over me."

Your body is craving nourishment, healing and nutritious food. Today, make it a point to eat foods that make you feel good about yourself and avoid chemicals, artificial and processed foods.

"I fill my body with clean and nutritious foods in order to protect, heal and nourish my body. With every bite I know that I am getting stronger and healthier."

There is a truth inside your soul that must be honored. Today work on honoring your truth and admitting to yourself how you really feel about a certain situation or event. Even though the truth can stir up fears it can also set you free.

"I honor my highest truth and know that it is safe to express how I truly feel."

Today is the day to venture out of your comfort zone and to try something new. While your comfort zone has been kind to you, perhaps it has also been blocking you from reaching new heights. Aim to try something new or do something differently and see what inspiration it can offer you.

"It is safe for me to step out of my comfort zone in order to experience new and inspiring things."

Sometimes we can allow our minds to make things seem bigger and more important than they are, which makes things feel more stressful than they need to be. Today, work on adjusting your expectations and try to view things with a simpler perspective.

"Things are not as complicated as they seem, today I take a simpler approach to problem solving and trust that things will work out without my constant interference."

What you judge in others you are really judging in yourself. Practicing compassion and removing the need to judge will help you to see that everyone is just doing the best they can with what they know. This will also help you to release any judgements you have about yourself.

"I release all judgements about myself and others and know that everyone, including me is just doing the best they can."

Sometimes your heart has to break in order for it to open to the light. Your heart may be in need of some healing today. Be gentle with yourself and know that while you heart is precious, in order for it to open fully it must be willing to break.

"I am proud of myself for opening my heart and allowing the light in. It is through this light that I know I can truly heal and step onto the path of pure consciousness."

Being in the company of good friends can make everything feel better. Today, spend time with people who make you feel good. Bring some lightness into your day and watch how your fears and troubles just melt away.

"I am light. I am joy. Today I surround myself with people who have my best interest at heart and who lift me higher."

Stagnant energy can leave you feeling stuck, unmotivated and confused on how to proceed forward. Today, start moving your energy around through deep breathing, exercise and stretching. Make it a priority to get your energy moving again and see how neatly all the answers you have been seeking will unfold.

"I move my body in ways that make me feel vibrant, healthy and full of life. I take deep breaths to welcome in a new, fresh energy."

It is never too late to go after your passions. Today is all about bringing your greatest dreams and wishes into reality. Make a plan and get working for you will be supported on the road ahead.

"I know I hold the power, knowledge and wisdom to turn my greatest dreams into a reality. Nothing is impossible."

The Universe has been presenting you many opportunities to stand tall and step into your true personal power. Where in your life have you been acting small? Where in your life have you not been living up to your fullest potential? Today, allow the Universe to step in and show you just how powerful you really are.

"I am a powerful being who can handle all that the Universe delivers to me. Today, I step up and honour that I no longer have to act small in order to get by and that I can live up to my fullest potential."

Spending time in nature is the perfect way to recharge your batteries and provide you with fresh inspiration. Today, all the answers you seek can be found out in nature. Take the time to just be in the great outdoors and trust that the right inspiration will be delivered to you at the right time.

"I allow my body, mind and soul to heal in nature and know that the infinite wisdom of the natural world around me will always be my guide."

You are safe and protected as you move through this world. Know that you are never alone and that you are always covered in the light of the Divine. If you are feeling isolated or lonely, know that all you need to do is open your arms to receiving.

"I am protected by the Divine light of the Universe. I am safe and looked after in this world."

Your life is calling on you to take more risks and be more daring. You must trust yourself and take a leap of faith. Seek out your adventurous side today and see what rewards it brings you.

"I trust myself and my inner wisdom. Everyday I am opening my heart to taking a leap of faith in order to move forward."

The goddess of healing is on your side today. She is sending you positive beams of white light straight into your soul in order to heal your pains and sorrows. Open yourself to receive her blessings and watch your body transform.

"I am open to receiving the many blessings of healing delivered to me by the power of the Universe."

You know in your heart what is true. Stop doubting yourself and your decisions. Today, stand up for what you know to be right. Stand up for your truth and see how it changes the outcome.

"It is safe for me to express my truth for when I do, everything is as it should be and the outcome is always for my highest good."

You have all you need to manifest your dreams into a reality. Trust in yourself and know that you have everything you need in order to move forward. The time to act is now.

"I am a powerful co-creator of my destiny and within me and around me I hold all the tools I need to turn my dreams into realities."

There is abundance coming your way today. All you need to do is open your arms to receiving it and be grateful for your many blessings. .

"I am always receiving blessings of abundance from the Universe in beautiful and creative ways."

A confused mind can never make a wise decision. Today, focus on finding clarity and peace in your own mind before you think about moving forward. Trust that your best decisions will be made from a place of centred ease and grace.

"As I clear and still my mind it becomes a clear channel for receiving guidance and clarity on all situations."

Your soul has weathered many storms. Even though things have been chaotic around you, trust that your journey with this is now coming to an end. Your transformation is nearly complete. Eventually, you will be able to see everything as a blessing.

"I trust that all changes and transformations are happening for my highest good and that everything is unfolding perfectly."

It is time to ask those around you for help and guidance. You are not in this alone. Today, ask for help from those around you and watch how your life begins to fill with ease.

"I gracefully accept the help of those around me in order to release the weight I have been carrying. I do not need to do this alone."

Your body, mind and soul are in need of some cleansing. Take some time out today to purify your body from negative thoughts and toxins. Visualise yourself surrounded in a white light and see it melt away the clutter.

"My body, mind and soul is cleansed and restored with a healing, positive, white light."

It is time to reconnect with your family. Your family hold an ancient wisdom and a love for you that is strong. Today, consider reaching out to your family and expressing gratitude for their presence in your life. A family member who has crossed over may also be sending you a blessing today.

"I am grateful for my family and all of the love and wisdom they have provided me."

Spirit has been calling your name, will you answer? Spirit wants to deepen its connection with you in order to bring you comfort and guidance moving forward. You are destined for great things, allow Spirit in to guide you the way.

"I open my heart to the source energy, to the Divine Spirit energy that lives inside me and all around me. As I do, I feel a strong sense of connection and knowing of my purpose."

Today is a day for miracles! Expect the best possible outcome for yourself today and see how the entire Universe comes together to help you achieve it. Don't be afraid to dream big today and open yourself up to the infinite possibilities on offer.

"Miracles are happening all around me as I expand my awareness into the amazing limitlessness potential of this infinite Universe."

The human heart is your engine, fuel it with love and compassion and in return it will provide you with abundance, inspiration and the joy of life itself.

"I am fuelling my heart with love and compassion for myself, for others and for the world around me."

Be at peace with yourself and your body. Know that you are beautiful and perfect just the way you are. Today, instead of focusing on changing your body, consider accepting it just the way that it is. Learn to love your flaws and find the beauty in all that you see in your reflection.

"I am beautiful and perfect just the way I am, I love and respect my body and am grateful for all that it has provided me with."

You must ground your energy now in order to move forward. You must reconnect yourself with the earth and find a way to center your energy in order to feel balanced and calm.

"As I stand on this solid ground I feel my body rooted and centred. I feel the weight of my body supported by Mother Earth and through this feeling, I find my balance."

Are you hiding your thoughts and feelings out of fear?
Today, you must speak your truth, you must give your
thoughts and feelings a voice, you must express yourself.

*"It is safe for me to express myself and state my opinion. I will
no longer guard myself or hold myself back because of my
fears."*

It is time for you to surrender to all that is around you and join the flow and rhythm of life. When you do, you will be given the springs to leap forward and start a new chapter of adventure.

"As I surrender to the Universe, the steps I need to take in order to move forward become crystal clear."

It is time to take your focus away from others and onto yourself. You have been giving too much of your time and energy to others and have been neglecting your own well being. Today, pay attention to your own thoughts and feelings and don't hesitate to put your own needs before others.

"Today I give myself permission to put my own needs first. Today I will honor all that I am and respect my own boundaries. In doing so, I know that I will be able to serve others better."

Your soul didn't sign up for easy, your soul signed up for growth. It signed up to be ripped open and challenged. It signed up to learn how to love and be loved on the deepest of levels. If things have been challenging lately, remember this and know that everything is part of your path.

"When I look at the bigger picture I understand that all events around me are here to challenge me for my highest good."

When you allow fear to rule, you feel tightness, a regret, a heaviness. When you act from a place of love however, you feel a joy, a river, a flow moving within you that brings lightness and ease. Today, reflect on where you are making even your smallest decisions from- it from a place of love or fear?

"I free myself from my fears and use love instead to make all decisions in my life whether big or small."

There is an amazing source of strength being sent your way by the Universe today. Use this strength to step up and step in to the fullness of your being. Allow this strength to guide you to who you really are.

"I feel strong, I feel confident in my body and in my mind and through this strength I embrace myself for all that I am."

Don't stress about the future or the past, live in the now and know that things have a way of working out in time. Know that with minimal effort you will be guided with ease and grace.

"As I bring my awareness to the present moment everything becomes clear and I realize that I am supported by life."

Today and everyday you are held in the hands of the Universe. You are supported in the hands of the Universe and are protected by everything in this Universe. You are so cared for and loved that all you need to do is sit back and relax.

"All around me I feel the infinite love and support of the Universe. I am safe, I am loved and I am protected."

Patience is not just about waiting, it is about waiting with a good attitude. An attitude that everything is unfolding at the right time, in the right place and in the right way.

"I trust in the Divine timing of the Universe and know that all is unfolding as it needs to for my highest good."

We are creating our future in every moment. All of our thoughts, actions, words, energy and vibration are always being collected into a seed that will sprout into our future.

"I am a powerful co-creator of my destiny and every moment I am creating the most desirable future for myself."

Gratitude is the key to a happy and fulfilled life. The quickest way to cleanse your spirit and recalibrate your energy is to celebrate and really feel all that you are grateful for in your life.

"I am so grateful for the many blessings in my life and feel a pure joy when I celebrate them."

There is a trail of breadcrumbs that is always illuminating your way forward. Today, pay attention to the signs around you and watch how nature is always guiding you to your next best step.

"Today I open my eyes to the world around me and trust in the signs and intuition that I receive."

You are enough. Everything about you is enough. You have enough, you are enough, you just being here is enough. And that is truly wonderful.

"I am enough just as I am. My presence is enough just as it is. I am perfect just as I am."

Love is everywhere just waiting to be tapped into. In order to find love in your life you must welcome it. You must create and nurture space for love in your life by loving yourself.

"I love myself and my life and with this love I create space for more."

Today, set a goal to create more happiness in your life. Start planting small seeds of joy and watch how they burst into flowers in the garden of your soul. Make that your goal and everything else will fall into place.

"I create my own happiness through finding joy and gratitude in every moment of every day."

Everything you need is already inside of you. All you need to do is unlock the Universe that dwells within and start creating with what you find.

"I hold the power of the Universe inside of me. Everything I need can be found from within."

Today is a day to fill up your cup. To fill it with things of the self; self-love, self-worth and self-acceptance. Fill your cup until it overflows and spills out to touch the earth and the sky.

"I am a radiant and confident being who is loving myself more and more each day."

Wrap yourself in your arms and give yourself a hug of acceptance. Accept and forgive yourself, release your guilt and know that every day is an opportunity to start fresh.

"I embrace and love all that I am. I show myself compassion and forgive myself for all that I once believed was not good enough. I accept myself."

Today is a day for the soul, a day to let go, expand and open your heart to the miracles and blessings of the Universe. Pay attention to any signs you receive today, as they are surely to point you in the right direction.

"My heart is open to receiving all intuitive messages and blessings that are pouring in from the Universe."

The language of your soul is music. Your music. The beat of your rhythm and energy. To know joy is to know your soul. Today, welcome in the intelligence of your soul and let it guide you to your own rhythm.

"The more I stay true to myself the more my life flows with grace and ease."

The rustling of the leaves of a tree is not just the wind. It is the wind whispering secrets to the trees that laugh and respond in turn. The whole earth is alive with wisdom. Only when you silence your mind can you join back in the rhythm.

"As I still my mind, the wisdom of my soul emerges. As I open my eyes, my heart opens its door and I am one with the Universe."

Being present allows you to strip yourself of anxieties for the future and stresses of the past. Being present is a gift not only to others, but also to yourself.

"I move through the day with presence and carefree grace, knowing that all my needs are taken care of."

Sometimes it is only through feeling and exploring every last drop of fear, pain and joy that you truly allow yourself to open to clarity and purpose. Let yourself crack open, give yourself permission to feel, for when you do, all matters of the heart will become clear.

"As I release my pains and burdens I feel a sense of relief and healing. I am safe and protected as I allow myself to feel."

Set your intention from your heart. Plant it like a seed. Water and nourish it but also give it room to breathe. And then, when the timing is right it will blossom, like all things in nature do.

"I nurture my dreams and wishes in the hands of the Divine and trust that everything is unfolding perfectly."

Visit www.foreverconscious.com for more inspiration.

22564081R00040

Made in the USA
Columbia, SC
28 July 2018